Catalyst

Catalyst Solutions | Catalyst Career Partners, LLC
Life . Purpose . Career . Passion . Living Well

WIN THE CAREER GAME NOW!!

WIN THE CAREER GAME,
THE MOST IMPORTANT GAME IN YOUR LIFE.

FINISH

Millennial Edition

Find Your Career Purpose and Life Passion
NOW
Proven Tools and Tactics Give You the Edge

"WIN THE CAREER GAME NOW!! MILLENNIAL EDITION ©"
is a trademark/brand of Catalyst Career Partners LLC and
Winfred (Win) Deal, denoting a series of products that may
include but is not limited to books, blogs, podcasts, webinars,
articles, and digital content.

© 2015, 2016 Catalyst Career Solutions, LLC

1

Published by:

Catalyst Career Partners, LLC

2707 S. Newark Court

Aurora, CO 80014

720.313.8474

Copyright © 2015, 2016

Order Information: To order more copies of this book or to receive a complete catalog of other products by Winfred (Win) Deal contact:

Catalyst Career Partners, LLC

by calling

720.313.8474

What Clients say About Winfred and *WIN THE CAREER GAME NOW!!*

"Win was a major influence in my landing of an excellent unpublished position with a Fortune 500 company. He provided me with "hands-on" training on how to successfully contact decision-makers. He doesn't just tell you what you should do; he shows you how to do it."
Tom Nelson – Agilent

"I wholeheartedly recommend your proactive aggressive approach to launching job search campaigns. I am comfortable in the knowledge that, even if this present opportunity should not succeed, that I will have an effective and confident means to again pursue new career opportunities."
David Wilson, Hewlett Packard

"I had an opportunity to work with Win at a decision point in my personal development. Win has a way of distilling the critical elements out of a lot of information, communicating his insights clearly, staying focused on a project, and being a good guy to be around. He carefully blends personal experience, current technology and common sense into thoughtful, relevant suggestions. I enjoyed working with Win."
Chuck Caswell, Caswell Risk Advisory

"I had the pleasure of working with Win during my recent career transition. Win is extremely knowledgeable in his field and approaches every situation with a positive attitude. He provides excellent coaching and detailed planning during a career transition. His positive can do attitude is contagious and makes working with him a real pleasure. I definitely recommend Win. His knowledge, experience, and attitude will absolutely enhance your career transition experience."
Joe McNew

"I had an opportunity to work with Win at a decision point in my personal career. Win has the ability to communicate his ideas clearly, stays focused on the job at hand, and has a very engaging personality. He carefully blends personal experience, current technology and common sense into thoughtful suggestions. I enjoyed working with Win and would recommend him to others."
Lin Stark, CPA, MBA

Dedication

To my wife, Cheryl, who has been my rock and support through thick and thin. Thanks for everything.

A special Thank You
to those who helped make this book possible....
Thousands of Clients, who helped me learn critical life lessons

Contents

Introduction

This book represents nearly 20 years of hard work, experience and the efforts of many partners, "teammates" and clients. Maybe you're one of them!

I wanted to take a moment to share some thoughts with you about what to expect in this book.

First, it's interactive. There are many opportunities and exercises for you to go deeper in the content, gain access to several free training videos, audio books, blogs and podcasts and register to get updates to this book as it grows and I correct the inevitable errors, grammar and spelling mistakes, that are bound to occur.

In fact, if you find any mistakes, **PLEASE** tell me by sending the error and page you found it on to my email catalyst.winfred@gmail.com. Thanks in advance.

Second, this book is about proactive and positive action to generate your best and most successful career. It is for activists who are willing to do the uncomfortable things until they succeed. It isn't intended for those who want to sit on the sidelines in the Game of Life. The key word is "PLAY."

Third, this book is designed to start a conversation with you, give us a chance to get to know each other, develop trust, a bond and ultimately help us decide if we should work in the future.

Fourth, this is a book that's packed with content, action steps of ideas and proven ideas to play and win the career game as soon as possible.

Defining the Game

"**There's nothing worse in life than to discover that you have climbed to the top of the ladder of success and find it's leaning against the wrong wall!**"
Pete Smythe,
Cowboy Philosopher

The goal of this book is to deliver knowledge and wisdom to you, the player in the **Career Game**; *so that you will make certain that your ladder of success is leaning against the RIGHT wall.*

The title of this book is ***Win the Career Game Now!!.*** A few definitions are in order:

If we look at various definitions of **GAME**, we find that most definitions include the ideas of structure, enjoyment, social interaction, and the challenge of competition. We see school curriculums increasingly use games as educational

tools since they provide a fun and engaging way to learn practical skills.

Life, in general, fits these criteria, so I'm not being frivolous when I use the game analogy. The Career Game is serious business... a serious game.

TOOLS are instruments that help us change our environments.

The terms **TACTIC** and **STRATEGY** are often confused. STRATEGY outlines the overall plan of achieving a goal. TACTICS involve all of the mechanics needed to accomplish the strategy.

Imagine Rory McIlroy, Bubba Watson or Lexi Thompson and Suzanne Pettersen putting with a tennis racket or Roger Federer and Serena Williams volleying a tennis ball with a six iron. Obviously, they'd be using the wrong tool for the game they're playing. It would definitely have an impact on their results.

The unspoken thought of this book is, *"When You're Playing the Wrong Game, It Doesn't Matter How Good You Are."* **"You Can't Win."** It's amazing how often we try to play the "Game of Life" or various other games with the wrong tool when, in reality, we don't have to.

Knowing your career passion and life purpose simplifies playing the game and will help you become a more effective and powerful player. *The sooner you learn your life purpose and career passion; the sooner you will be able to minimize learning by PAINFUL experience.* Note that I emphasize the word minimize in the preceding sentence. Fortunately, or unfortunately life is about learning and making mistakes.

"You have to learn the rules of the game and then you have to play better than anyone else."
Albert Einstein.

I've always envied my oldest daughter, Jessica, because she knew in the eighth grade that she was going to be a veterinarian. Everything she did from that point forward was ultimately focused on doing what it took to become a veterinarian. She cleaned cages and walked dogs. No task was too insignificant in her learning process. It was and is, indeed, her career passion and life purpose.

I, on the other hand, took 30 years to figure it out. I am my own best example of learning from experience. Learning from experience can be very painful and quite expensive. My parents were teachers and I decided early on that I did not want to be a teacher. Other than that I had no idea about what I was going to do.

A good student and class leader in high school, I was accepted to Duke University. I became a history major without any planning for the future and what I might do. I was a diligent but not spectacular student. I graduated in four years and entered the US Air Force. It seemed like something that could be of interest as a career and it actually was. I was a B-52 instructor navigator on a combat crew in the Vietnam era.

It took a while, but I came to realize that the Air Force was not to be my future. I received a Master's in management while on active duty. I completed my five-year Air Force commitment and entered the private sector still not knowing what my purpose and passion in life was. I had no idea what I wanted to do when I "grew up."

I started my business career in management training with a $1B manufacturing company, the Gates Rubber Company, and lasted one year. I had no passion for the product (V-belts and hydraulic hose, and automobiles in general held no "magic" for me). Over time I tried financial services, retail, mortgage banking, property management, politics, advertising sales, commercial loan brokerage, and career marketing and coaching.

Naturally, career marketing and coaching are really all about teaching, facilitating and transformation! When I finally came to understand what I do best and love the most is career marketing and helping clients identify their life purpose and career passion and the highest and best use of their skills and abilities, I knew I was "home."

"Life" will sometimes determine that your purpose and passion will change and that is just fine. It's better to have a purpose and passion now as a Millennial starting out than flounder around for years not really understanding what you do best.

I am an absolute believer that it is better to figure it out for the "now" and move forward based on that knowledge. Chuck Blakeman of the Crankset Group put it very well when he shared his Marine Corps soccer team's motto, "**Bad plans carried out violently many times yield good results. Do something**."

Life purpose and career passion give you the ability to overcome incredible obstacles that will be placed in front of you as you move forward in your life and career. While I am not a believer in striving to achieve perfection, Steve Jobs of Apple certainly managed to build a company based on his vision of perfection. I can definitely say that had I the capabilities to work for Apple I could not have worked for Steve Jobs. Life is too short.

"Winning is a result of a strong purpose and passion supporting a persistence that leads to a "laser like" focused action"
Steve Jobs

A meaningful definition of "win" is to "gain by labor, effort or struggle." Notice that this definition of winning does not entail driving your competitors into the ground or doing "whatever it takes" -- i.e., lying, cheating, etc. (as we see via "Reality TV".

Years ago, Porsche ran an ad which summarizes what winning is all about superbly when they stated,

"When w**e learn from the effort, the struggle and from each success and each failure, and improve ourselves through the experience, we will have fulfilled our potential and played well."**
Porsche Advertisement

The **Game of Life** is the ultimate game. It is the only game that has the same beginning and the same end for all of us. We cannot control either the events of birth or the happenstance of death. It can be glorious or mundane. It is what is. It is "reality."

The key, the essence, is to learn from the activity of the game, to absorb the value, to learn the lesson, and to get better. Nobody says it better than Michael Jordan in the following quote:

> *"I've missed over 9,000 shots in my career.*
> *I've lost almost 300 games.*
> *26 times I've been trusted to take the game winning shot... and missed.*
> *I've failed over and over and over again in my life.*
> *And that is why I succeed."*
> **Michael Jordan**

Not a bad record for someone who was cut from his high school basketball team! Michael's passion would not let him stop getting better and learning and mastering the game. Failure was not acceptable.

I am totally in alignment with the Porsche and Michael Jordan statements above. The key to true success in life is to learn from the experience and apply the lessons you learn in future games.

> *"Winning or not winning indicates that we have completed one game, and are ready to move on to the next one. Then we must move on."*
> **Porsche Advertisement**

One of the most powerful influences on my career was politics. I started at the "grass roots" level knocking on doors and delivering literature. For over 10 years, I became increasingly involved beginning with knocking on doors and eventually my involvement increased and I "graduated" to managing both successful as well as unsuccessful campaigns.

I discovered that the Career Game **is** identical to a political campaign. You are the candidate. You have a purpose or a goal, which is to win and then build on your life purpose and passion in life to make yourself, your family, and society better.

> *As part of the planning and preparation process, you must understand your purpose and passions and how they impact your personal balance sheet, assets and liabilities.*

The awareness of *the good, the bad and the ugly* is critical. **"Reality" is what matters.** It's just as important to be able to counter liabilities, as it is to speak of assets. The game is about **BUILDING PERSONAL VALUE**...for presentation to, and selection by, the electorate or the hiring manager/decision maker.

The **final step is ACTION and PERSISTENCE. Get face to face**. *CONNECTING* is the key word. The magic

happens when you are face to face. Press the flesh. Go door to door. Talk to people. **Let them know what you stand for. Persist. PLAY FULL ON to the end of the game**. Give it your all. **When you have identified your life purpose, this process becomes infinitely simpler**.

As you move forward, recruit and connect with your team, you will discover that people will help. In fact, people you don't know are waiting to help. It's a very real positive validation that people are good. Coming in second has been compared to "kissing your sister." One good thing about the *Career Game* (all games really) is that you do gain a benefit from participating." Your effort matters and will make you better the next time as you learn from your experience.

So, the purpose of this book is to help you *Win the Career Game Now!!* and experience and the **Career Game** as a "relatively more enjoyable" process. By "relatively more enjoyable" I mean you will receive more "yes's" than "no's." Remember: It only takes one accepted offer to get out of the unfun Career Search Game and it might be a result of your next call.

The key "tactic" is to identify, speak to, and CONNECT with people who will become teammates and help you through the game. Building your team makes play simpler and infinitely faster to complete. It also helps to build momentum as you play.

Win the Career Game Now!! is about moving from paper to people. It is about *PROACTIVE and FOCUSED ACTION* **using power tools and action tactics.** In addressing your Millennial Career Game, we will spend virtually no time addressing the issues of resumes, cover letters, and other passive tools. Instead, we will **focus on goal-oriented action and the proactive tools that will help**

you identify your career purpose and passion in record time by connecting with the right people.

One of the most effective **Power Tools** is *LinkedIn*. As we move forward, you will see how LinkedIn very specifically (and other social media and "apps" in general) multiply the effectiveness and power of the strategies we will discuss. I began developing the power tools idea and giving workshops in the early 1990s and self-published the first volume as *Power Tools and Action Strategies* in 2005.

The **tactics** and **tools** mentioned have always worked wonderfully. I didn't even mention LinkedIn in the first volume because it was so new. The good news is LinkedIn, since its inception in 2002, has put my ideas on steroids and magnified the ease and effectiveness of **CONNECTING** by an order of magnitude.

As long as you are **CONNECTING DIRECTLY** with people, doing the things we recommend and in the manner they are meant to be used, ***WE GUARANTEE YOU WILL BE A WINNER, YOU WILL FIND YOUR PURPOSE AND PASSION***.

This is not rocket science. ***It's very simple... it's very straightforward... and it's not really painful!***

Play to Win the Career Game

The following testimonial from David Wilson, a client who played the Career Search segment of the Career Game very effectively. His story illustrates the essence of playing the career search game well. In it, David speaks to the frustrations that most players in the game experience prior to learning the techniques presented in this book. He understood the necessity of being proactive in the game. He learned that these simple, but not necessarily easy, techniques and processes really work. In fact, every aspect of his testimonial will be used to illustrate various points as we move through this book. I hope each and every one of you will succeed as David did.

Dear Win:

> *Greetings! I hope you will take the opportunity to share my successful and personally fulfilling experience with your Wednesday seminar groups and future clients.*
>
> *After attending your seminar, I realized that my own personal job search campaign was far too dependent on resumes, written solicitations, and wishful responses to misleading classified ads. In fact, I*

submitted resumes to about ten promising positions in Colorado Springs, including two that I found out about through my position at Peat Marwick. All returned the same response; I would be considered, and if I were not a short-list interview candidate, would be put on file for six months. I never heard from any of these opportunities again.

The new word for my job search vocabulary was "proactive." To all who have inquired about this successful experience, I have responded that what was required was to "get out there and do it" instead of "staying home" and thinking that opportunity will come knocking.

You and I spent two hours on the phone, completing about thirty calls, all intended towards informational interviews. In fact, you even made two of the calls on my behalf, pretending to be me. The first was where you left a voice mail with the CEO. The second resulted in an informational interview with a Colorado Springs architect. My own phone calling established four more informational interviews.

Let me make this point: of all the hours spent with you, with the computer, with the library, and with my own thoughts, these two were the most difficult and the most successful. Talking to presidents, CEO's, screeners, and even receptionists is difficult when you know in your mind you are pursuing a job. The script is invaluable. I found myself far more comfortable after ten calls than after one.

The interview with the CEO resulted in my position. The other four interviews were not ten minutes, but over an hour each, and resulted in over twenty contacts throughout Colorado Springs. I never needed to pursue these contacts, but the system proved itself by giving me an excellent set of backup options. Keep in mind; every one of those backup options would have had the benefit of a referral. That's a far cry from the earlier "cold calls."

The informational interview with Telephone Express was supposed to be just that; I was an architect talking to a telecommunications company. I thought there would be no common ground.

However, when talking to the CEO, not only do you find out about all opportunities within the company, you may even convince him/her to create new ones. The latter was my opportunity. My department staffing skills and significant computer experience became as attractive a contribution to telecommunications as they were to airport planning.

After thirty minutes of sizing each other up, the CEO and I were walking down the hall to meet the Director of Corporate

Development. After 30 minutes with the Director of Corporate Development, I was going to lunch with the Director of Customer Service. After lunch, I was brought back to schedule interviews with the Call Center Staffing Supervisor and Director of Technical Support. All of these interviews were my opportunity to sell these individuals on a position that the CEO and I had patched together just hours earlier.

One week later I was called for my references. The following week I was offered a job at a progressive salary that within 9 months will match what I was being paid in California. I became an ACD Coordinator, a position that is divided equally between call distributor software management, and call center staffing analysis. A position that did not exist prior to my arrival.

One final note: I did have something in common with the CEO, we both went to the University of Notre Dame. However, I don't believe that is the reason he called me back. Rather, I did some library work, and saw that he was mentioned in "People in the News" in the Colorado Springs Business Journal. I think by acknowledging that bit of research in my voice mail to him, I projected a sense of sincere interest in his company, and an effort to be more than just another guy after a job. It surely made the voice mail more interesting than, "Hi, I'd like to meet you."

I wholeheartedly recommend our proactive aggressive approach to launching job search campaigns. I am comfortable in the knowledge that, even if this present opportunity should not succeed, that I will have an effective and confident means to again pursue new career opportunities.

Sincerely,
David Wilson.

For valuable resource tools and tactics to help you move forward in all variations of the Career Game, visit:
www.winthecareergamenow.com/resources

Five Natural Laws for *Winning the Career Search Game*

Natural Law # 1: Be Prepared to Play

You Must Understand Yourself - Personal Assessment

It's crucial to have an understanding of "who you are" in this process. There are many personality profiles including the Core Values Index (CVI) by Taylor Protocols (In fact, I recommend you take the CVI using this link, http://bit.ly/1wKGjKB. It's free, takes 10 minutes and gives you instant feedback in the form of a 3 minute video and 4-5 pages of written material. It will give you an excellent idea of what your personal "wiring" is, and how it impacts your communications and relationships with others.

This is a worthwhile exercise-- in fact, consider it mandatory--and you should find a way to complete a profile if you haven't completed one to date. Many other assessments are available online today. In Exercise 1 (p. 35), we will examine how taking one of these personal assessments benefits you in discovering your passion, purpose, and your brand.

Why Must I Brand Myself?

Realize that *job boards are a black hole*. The **good news is you now have access to every published job opening in the world**! The bad news is so does everyone else!

No wonder human resource professionals don't have time to respond to every job seeker. They don't have time. As a result of screening software or Applicant Tracking Software (ATS), if you do not have a perfect, literally perfect, background match to the requirements of the ad and key words, **you will be screened out without a real person seeing your resume 99% of the time**.

- It is stunning to me, but many job seekers are fixated on job boards and posting resumes. Then, for some reason, they become frustrated and depressed because they get no response or feedback. They actually believe they are the victims of discrimination.

- You are being selected out because you do not match the job description 100 percent. You are being screened without a human being seeing your ad response or any creative materials. To respond to a job advertisement today without having a 100% match is a study in futility. In the old days (5 to 10 years ago! Or two months ago!) there might be "only" 300 people responding to an ad, today there will be a minimum of 3,000. Consider the fact that 30 million (conservatively) resumes are in play monthly in the United States alone.

The greatest issue, of course, is that by using screening software the human element is lost in the job search process and ultimately that will hurt more than help companies who depend on finding new employees through the web in the future. This is reality and likely will not change.

- In today's career search world, using social media networks is mandatory to an effective proactive campaign and should be your main focus of time rather than more traditional job boards.
- It is equally important that your creative materials (resumes, letters, etc.) and your online image be consistent and congruent. One must definitely leverage the other.
- Joshua Waldman, author of *Job Searching with Social Media for Dummies*, makes comments that are right on the mark:

    "But what typically happens to job seekers is, they willy-nilly start filling in profiles without regard to consistency and impact. Recruiters find inconsistent people a risk and put them into the maybe pile. That means your resume, LI profile, FB posts, in fact, everything should feel as if it came from the same person."

With a minimum of 80% of available jobs today being "unlisted/unpublished/nonpublished," connecting online with the appropriate decision maker has become more important than ever before. In a recent poll, tens of millions of Americans indicated that their jobs came from using some type of social network.

- Remember that social media is a publishing tool. When you use it, you are a publisher-- details about your personal brand. Social media is one of the tools you will use to market and advertise your abilities and skills. You must think about the image you are portraying and how it will impact your life.
- To avoid the "maybe" pile, having a consistent brand is essential.

Your Brand

I think the more important task for a young person than developing a personal brand is figuring out what she's great at, what she loves to do, and how she can use that to leave an imprint in the world. Those are tough questions, but essential ones. Answer those - and the personal brand follows.

Daniel H. Pink

Every day we are bombarded with about 5,000 brand messages. What kind of brand messages did you hear today? (Progressive Insurance, "Swoosh," car brands, business cards...).

The job of marketing is to get someone to pay attention to you.

In 2013, over 10 million Americans found work through LinkedIn.

This brings us to the definitions of Marketing and Branding and Advertising. In our "Game," when the target decision maker has need of your product or service, we want him or her to think of YOU, and that target is always the hiring manager. It is **NEVER** an HR person in your target company. Some of my best friends and former clients are HR professionals. Having said that, unless you are seeking a job in human resources, an HR professional is **NEVER** the appropriate decision maker.

- **Key Definitions**:

  *__Advertising__ is about getting your attention.

  *__Marketing__ is about renting out space in the mind of the consumer.

*A **brand** is what you put in that space. It's the promise you make.

YOUR BRAND is a way to connect with you--your promise of what you bring to your next employer. Your brand includes: identity, visual, logo, name, emotional image, it's what people think of when they hear or read your name, it's a way to connect to you.

- **Example:** Think about how branding started out. It was on cattle. So if you have a whole field of unidentified bovines/cows, how can you tell if my cows get into your fields, how can you tell my cows from your cows?

  You can't. So you take this hot branding iron and brand them. So think about this if you have a whole bunch of people that have the same type of service that you do. For example, 1000s of people in your city do Information Technology.

How do you separate yourself from the rest of them? You promise them something. It's this whole identity. When someone comes to you they have this whole idea of what you're promising them and what they are going to get from you.

- Many people fill out online profiles without first thinking about the brand promises they are making in these profiles/resumes. **If you want to succeed at the job search, first determine your brand.**

Consider the following brands:

- Oprah
    - Born into poverty and built her career out of huge adversity
    - Uses her personal influence for good
    - Epitomizes human strength and character
- Steve Jobs
    - Think differently
    - Innovate

- Hard pressing
- Perfectionist
- Revolutionary

The You/Them model of personal branding

Now that you have an intuition about personal branding, and can probably spot a personal brand when you see it, we need to define this in a way that you can work with as a job seeker. Rather than keeping this idea in the realm of celebrities, realize that everyone in the world has a brand.

Brand or be Branded!

My greatest strength is common sense. I'm really a standard brand - like Campbell's tomato soup or Baker's chocolate.
Katharine Hepburn

- Your brand promise needs to be congruent with **YOU.** Just as market products such as pet food or detergent have to live up to their claims, when you share your brand with the world, you have to be 100% congruent with what you are saying.
- Next, your brand promise will need to resonate with the interests of your target organization: **THEM.**
  - Through research, you can learn exactly what these companies are looking for.

- Discovering their needs will help get their attention on you.

  All **serious** candidates are expected to know how they will **help** organizations **specifically.**

- Where the needs of an organization intersect with your specific ability to help is your personal brand.

  However, your message will fall short if you only do research.

You must also understand that...

- **Know**ing **your value** is the first part of getting congruent with your brand. This helps you:
  - Make decisions about what companies you would or wouldn't work for.
  - Decide what roles you would be willing to accept and for what money.
  - Makes you more believable when you talk about yourself.

- So we start off with a series of introspective exercises that will help you articulate who you are in a clearer way. The activities that follow will help you complete the YOU/THEM model of your own personal brand.

For valuable resource tools and tactics to help you move forward in all variations of the Career Game, visit:
www.winthecareergamenow.com/resources

Exercise 1: Personality Profile

1. **Explore:** Find an online personality profile such as the Core Values Index by Taylor Protocols (as mentioned above: http://bit.ly/1wKGjKB). You will also be able to easily find websites that offer free assessments and broad interpretations of your results.

2. **Reflect:** According to your profile results (and what you know about yourself),

   What are the main qualities of your personality type results?

   - How does your personality type prefer to tackle projects?
   - Do you prefer to work in a group with other people, or more autonomously?
   - Do you like to have clear direction, or do you thrive on the unexpected?
   - Do you prefer to work intuitively ("go with your gut"), or do you prefer established procedures?
   - If provided (or going by what you know about yourself), what areas of improvement inherent to your personality type would, if modified,

help you meet with greater success? In other words, what challenges do you see?

- What situations drive you crazy?
- What situations make you feel alive?

Exercise 2: Your Values

Thanks to Joshua Waldman, author of *Job Searching with Social Media for Dummies* for this exercise.

You can't just ask someone what his or her values are. They exist in context and as such require a fun exercise to parse out. This exercise asks you to choose between things. The reason for your choice often reveals a core value.

Quickly review each of these exercises:

1. Choose from anyone in your life, people you know and admire, then select three. What were your three idols willing to sacrifice to achieve what they did?
2. Think of and list one to three successes you're most proud of.

3. What three core values do you see within these lists? What values surface as most important to you?

Exercise 3: Putting it Together: Understand Your Personal Balance Sheet

Once you understand the rules of the career game. It's important to understand the "good, the bad and the ugly" about yourself. This leads us to the personal balance sheet. It is important that all players in the game understand their strengths and weaknesses. We focus on functional, transferable, skills, and abilities. These are the capabilities that are required to successfully complete any task in the world of work.

For our purposes, we just want to make certain that you understand your assets and liabilities. This understanding is critical, because as you play the game you must be able to present yourself in the most favorable light at all times. Your ability to tell your story powerfully and concisely will be very much in your favor and make you a better competitor. You will also have to cover liability questions that arise. The game is about value building. From the balance sheet, campaign materials and the game plan are developed.

Using the information from Exercises 1 and 2, fill in the table below.

As you continue to incubate these ideas, come back to this table and refine your thoughts. Also make notes here about books you want to read or classes you might take to enhance your assets column.

Your Value Statement is your "elevator speech." What would you tell a decision maker of a company about yourself on the brief ride up an elevator with limited time to tell your story.

Assets	Liabilities
1.	1.
2.	2.
3.	3.
4.	4.
5.	5.

Owner's Equity (Your Value Statement)

Additional notes:

Exercise 4: The Reticular Activating System (How THEY find you)

Have you ever noticed how when you become interested in or buy a car, you start to see that car everywhere? Or if you're wearing a blue shirt, you notice everyone else wearing blue as well? These are examples of the Reticular

Activating System (RAS)—filtering portion of the brain--at work.

Hiring managers' brains work the same as yours: you need to speak to their top-of-mind problems. Get in their filters. They see a lot of resumes and profiles, but if your message talks about something they are already thinking about (painful issues in the company, etc.), they will definitely notice you.

How can you use this principle to improve your communications with companies?

1. **Research** to find out what current issues (pain or opportunity) a company you're interested in is facing.
2. **Identify** one or more of their problems that you feel uniquely qualified to handle.
3. **List** your assets and liabilities from the company's perspective.
4. **Compare** this list with the lists you made in Exercise 1.
5. **Evaluate:** What differences do you see when you look at your personal balance sheet from the employer's perspective?

For Whom Should I Work? Where to find THEM.

Thanks to the Johnson O'Connor Research Foundation (jocrf.org) for the following information on their Resources page:

> The United States government maintains several websites that provide helpful information to jobseekers and others who want to investigate career fields:
>
> **O*NET OnLine** was conceived by the U.S. Department of Labor to be the definitive resource for counselors, educators, human resource specialists, and the general public to learn more about occupations.
>
> **The Occupational Outlook Handbook** is a very useful guide, produced by the U.S. Department of Labor, with basic information about the most common career fields, job trends, educational requirements and more.
>
> America's Labor Market Information System, **CareerOneStop**, is a collection of sites that help people find jobs and learn about careers. It includes **America's Job Bank** and **Career InfoNet**.

The Johnson O'Connor Research Foundation also offers these other ideas...

- **Cooljobs.com** lists non-traditional postings, like circus performer or mystery shopper.
- **Coolworks.com** emphasizes outdoor jobs, especially short-term positions in travel and tourism.
- **EscapeArtist.com** is a site specializing in international listings.
- The **Freelancers Union** is a non-profit organization dedicated to the needs of freelancers, consultants and independent contractors.
- A good source of information about careers that don't require a college degree is the **Vocational Information Center**.

Major Job Boards

- Check out major job-posting sites, such as **HotJobs** (now part of Yahoo!), **Monster, MonsterTRAK, Careers.Org,** the **Recruiters Online Network**, and **America's Job Bank. SimplyHired** and Indeed.com are meta-search engines that will search many job-posting sites at once.
- Some job-posting sites are more focused. For example, **Idealist.org** is for not-for-profit listings

nationwide; the **FindLaw Career Center** specializes in the legal field; and **EnvironmentalCareer.com** , which highlights jobs which focus on improving the environment. There are countless others; a Google search may help you find them.

- Trade publication classifieds and professional organizations often have a section with job listings. **IEEE-USA** for engineers and **ChronicleCareers** by *The Chronicle of Higher Education* are two such sites.

- Most large companies post their openings on their website. For examples, see **Apple, Google,** or **Fidelity Investments**.

Where can I get more job search help?

The Johnson O'Connor Research Foundation offers more ideas:

- **JobHuntersBible.com** is a site maintained by Dick Bolles, as a supplement to his popular book *What Color is Your Parachute?*

- For students and recent college graduates, **CollegeGrad.com** has a variety of tools for the jobseeker.

- **The Riley Guide** is a directory of employment and career information sources and services on the Internet. It is primarily intended to provide instruction for job seekers on how to use the Internet to their best advantage.
- **WetFeet** is a site dedicated to "Helping you make smarter career decisions."
- **Quintessential Careers** offers comprehensive career and job-hunting advice, with a variety of articles, tools, tips, and tutorials.

SEO influenced Job Boards for the Millennial Job Seeker. From Josh Waldman's book *Job Searching with Social Media for Dummies* (2nd edition). Be aware that change is constant on the web and that some may well change or become nonfunctional.

- **LinkUp.com**: Finds and indexes jobs from the employer's own websites. Currently, the site indexes over 35,000 company's jobs sites.
- **Jojari.com**: Uses your LinkedIn profile or resume to conduct a more thorough search than traditional job-board searches.
- **Startwire.com**: Gives you status updates on the progress of your job application. Provides job matching, one-click apply and status updates. Be

aware that you might be linked to other job sites. We found that we joined four other sites (without our consent): ZipRecruiter, CareerAlerter, Beyond.com, and Glassdoor. At least they are good ones!

- **TweetMyJobs.com**: Brings the job market to Twitter.
- **Cachinko.com**. Leverages Facebook network. Tells you who is a good connection to the job you're applying for.

Exercise 5: Taking a look at what O*Net has to Offer

1. Go to https://www.onetonline.org/
2. Click on Find Occupations:

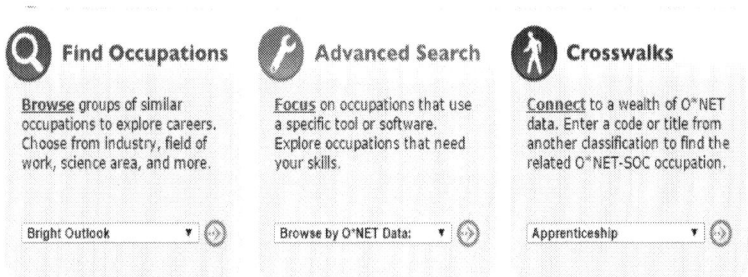

Find Occupations
Browse groups of similar occupations to explore careers. Choose from industry, field of work, science area, and more.

Bright Outlook ▼

Advanced Search
Focus on occupations that use a specific tool or software. Explore occupations that need your skills.

Browse by O*NET Data: ▼

Crosswalks
Connect to a wealth of O*NET data. Enter a code or title from another classification to find the related O*NET-SOC occupation.

Apprenticeship ▼

3. Explore the drop down menu in the Career Cluster section, and choose a career cluster that appeals to you.

4. Scroll through the results and choose three that appeal to you. Click on each and view what information you can acquire through the Summary Reports. Details, and Custom tabs for each.

5. Return to the Find Occupations page, and go to the Bright Outlook section. This section contains jobs projected to grow much faster than average. Choose three that appeal to you for now, and view what information you can acquire through the Summary Reports. Details, and Custom tabs for each.

6. Explore the Advanced Search and Crosswalk tabs on the main O*Net page in the same way.

7. What did you find most useful about this website? How could this website help you find your passion and purpose—or at least an industry or career worth exploring?

Have a Game Plan: Resumes, Letters, and an Identified Field of Play

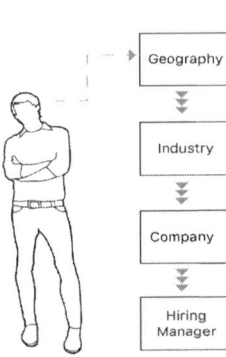

When the activities required in producing your personal balance sheet are completed, you are now ready to develop your game plan. Your resumes and any marketing materials will be completed from the results of your personal balance sheet.

Everyone in the career field has an opinion of resumes. *The Riley Guide* (www.rileyguide.com), updated and maintained by Margaret Dikel, is an absolutely marvelous online resource. It will answer questions that haven't occurred to you. (It is, in fact, a tremendous place to start with questions on virtually everything not covered in **Win the Career Game Now!!**). These written materials are very important to your game because they will support your activities at all times. They will not, however, get you the job you seek. I say again, they are support documents.

The realities discussed above provide a solid overview of the mindset you must have as you begin play. Most people really don't understand the rules or the realities of playing the career search game. This is very unfortunate but very much in our favor, as we will have a very clear picture of the playing field and how to effectively win the game.

In *WIN THE CAREER GAME NOW!!*, we are **always and only focused on the proactive game**. As we continue, we will speak of an action plan to help you set benchmarks and achieve your goals in the game. In some respects, you might consider it a marketing plan. The action plan will define channels of activity. But first let us consider the proactive vs. the passive channels of activity in the game.

For valuable resource tools and tactics to help you move forward in all variations of the Career Game, visit
www.winthecareergamenow.com/resources

Natural Law # 2: Understand the Marketing Plan

"A proactive campaign is one that is based on focused, positive action."

Key understanding: **you must be proactive.** As stated previously, nobody is going to effectively play the game for you. The Career Game is a team game. We are all part of a team; we are going to be building a team. We will be spending quite some time investigating the key elements of building a powerful support team. A team who will help you play the game much more effectively and put you on the winner's stand.

Remember what David said in his letter:

*After attending Win's seminar, I realized that my own personal **job search campaign was far too dependent on resumes, written solicitations, and wishful responses to misleading classified ads.** In fact, I submitted resumes to about ten promising positions in Colorado Springs, including two that I found out about through my position at Peat Marwick. All returned the same response; I would be considered, and if I were not a short-list interview candidate, would be put on file for six months. I never heard from any of these opportunities again.*

What David describes is very typical of the actions of players initially in the game: submitting resumes to positions for which they may or may not qualify, and then hoping and praying that they receive a call. It almost never happens.

Passive Channels and the Published Job Market

What do I mean by published job market?

Today's Published Job Market is 98% online. Printed ads are few and far between nowadays and mostly irrelevant. All ads, local or national, eventually end up online. This certainly makes them available to a much wider segment of job seekers. Web sites such as monster.com, careerbuilder.com, LinkedIn Jobs, SimplyHired, Craigslist and many, many other job sites offer literally thousands of job opportunities.

The good news is you will probably be able to find jobs that are exciting to you online. The bad news is so will thousands of other competitors. I have spoken with hundreds of human resource professionals over the years and all have said **that 10 percent of all responses to published help wanted ads have every job requirement they are looking for.**

Don't expect anyone to think. I

Especially don't expect a human resource professional to think outside the box when considering responses to ads. Neither should you. They don't have time. An Internet ad is **a passive channel** because **after you have responded to the ad there is virtually nothing you can do to make the process move more quickly, nothing**.

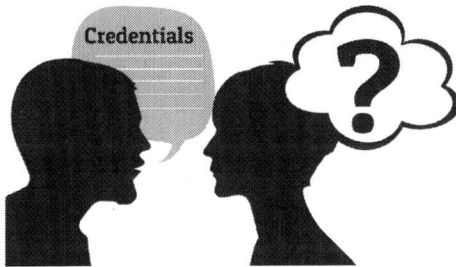

You are not dealing with a true decision maker when dealing with a human resource professional. They do not have the need and did not define the position. That does not mean they are not nice people, it means that they are not part of our team.

They have a job to do and that is to sort the responses and forward them to the decision maker with the need. Therefore from a mental attitude point of view do not expect a response unless you meet every specification of the ad.

Executive Recruiters. The second passive channel of activity is executive recruiters or headhunters. Typically, w**ith recruiters you must, repeat must, meet every criterion they seek.** Recruiters are given job orders to fill when a human resource department does not have the time or expertise to locate appropriate candidates.

It follows very clearly **that they are paid by the company** to provide candidates that an internal human resource department cannot handle. Therefore if there are 15 job requirements for the position, it is in their own interest to find candidates who possess every one of those requirements in the company's industry. It is difficult, if not impossible, for a recruiter to present a candidate who possesses no industry experience. Typically, recruiters will not help you change industries.

If you have strong qualifications it is possible to do a broadcast e-mail to recruiters on the Internet.

A recruiter will call you if there is an interest, but most likely you will receive no response. Under no circumstances are you to consider a recruiter as a true member of your team. The hiring Company employs them. If your skills meet company needs, a recruiter will work with you. If not, you will not receive return phone calls nor can you expect to reach them for a personal contact. The odds that they will refer you on to potential hiring company are slim.

Mass mailings. A mass mailing is considered a passive channel because you put it together and mail to every decision maker in a specific industry. It is possible that this could also be a mass e-mailing to specific decision makers should you be able to collect their e-mail address.

This is not an effective form of contact because of the general nature of the letter or e-mail. In today's market, only targeted emails and letters have any degree of effectiveness.

Control Your Actions. **Never expect a return phone call**. Your chances of receiving a response from a mass mailing are slim and none. However, you might get lucky if the stars are in alignment.

The Proactive Channels

There are essentially three proactive channels: targeted mailings, "change" mailings, and focused networking.

> **Targeted Mailing**. A targeted mailing will be tailored to meet the needs of a specific company and decision maker. Targeted letters and resumes require customization and quite some time to prepare. It will be required to complete relatively in-depth research to tailor these letters.

It is not likely that you would send out more than twenty-five targeted letters per week. The level of success with these letters is certainly better than a mass mailing. **Phone follow-up is required! To send a targeted mailing without an attempt at follow-up is a waste of time**.

"Positive Change" Mailing. Identifying "positive changes" can be very effective. If you see in a newspaper article or an Internet forum, that a company is growing, merging with other companies or having the challenges associated with positive change, they might have need for someone with your skills.

Therefore, a targeted letter or tailored resume can be sent to the appropriate decision maker detailing how you can help solve their problems. This is truly thinking outside the box and may certainly generate activity. A former client, Len Gilmore, noticed that a cable company was opening a new division.

His background was in high technology and not telecommunications (therefore he did not have "industry experience!") but he had a great skill set that would be very useful in a growing company. He sent a spot opportunity letter to the CEO tying his skills to the needs of a growing company and it generated four VP level interviews for him with key decision makers in the targeted cable company. Of any mail piece, the "positive change" letter is far and away the most effective. Phone follow-up is required.

Focused Networking/Connecting. Focused Networking/Connecting is what *WIN the Career Game Now!!* is all about. It is the most effective and most direct form of contact with a decision maker. Focused Networking/Connecting is quite different than networking as it is normally done. Focused networking will be covered in-depth later in this book.

A comprehensive campaign will include both passive and proactive channels. Our focus in *WIN THE CAREER GAME NOW!!* is on the proactive channels. We will not consider the elements that are critical to effective resumes and introductory letters.

There are many other resources available online and in libraries that very effectively cover those tools. Our goal is to develop strategies and techniques to directly identify and contact the decision maker without an intermediary.

For valuable resource tools and tactics to help you move forward in all variations of the Career Game, visit:
winthecareergamenow.com/resources

Natural Law # 3: Understand the Proactive Game

Develop Targets. The proactive campaign begins with deciding where geographically you want to live and work. You cannot effectively say, "I'm willing to go anywhere and do anything." It's too broad. The statement might be true, but there is no way you can conduct an effective proactive campaign with such a wide scope.

The reality is you actually have no focus. So, discuss it with your family and choose where you really want to live. In fact, choose your top three locations and use them to begin your planning. *Geography* is essential as the first step in choosing your targets.

Your second criterion, after geography, is *industry.* The assessments mentioned above will help you start your industry focus if you don't have one. Implementing informational interviewing as recommended in ***WIN THE CAREER GAME NOW!!*** will help you complete your search.

If you've identified an industry, wonderful. If you want to consider a new industry that also is wonderful. Your functional, transferable, skills and abilities will be of value in any industry and any company. In changing industries, however, you must be prepared to overcome the "lack of industry experience" objection consistently. In fact, that is an objection everyone must master at one time or another.

Seek positive change. Since you are the solution to some decision maker's problem/pain, I recommend you investigate growth companies and growth industries. While there is opportunity in a company that is downsizing, most often they are not looking to hire. The opportunities associated with positive change are usually much more enjoyable and have a longer term benefits to both yourself and the company.

Once an industry is selected, it is a simple process to identify companies in that industry in a particular geographic location. Many online resources are available at most libraries with no charge. LinkedIn is a fabulous resource in this regard as well.

You can sort your target companies by Standard Industrial Classification (SIC) or a variety of selection criteria like size of company, revenues, number of employees, and other variables. When the target company is identified we can find the appropriate decision maker. The Internet has made this process of identification of geography, industry, company, and decision maker an order of magnitude simpler than five years ago.

Targets also make your research more effective. It is impossible to do in-depth and effective research on thousands of companies on a national scale. By that I mean, if you don't have specific focused targets in a specific focused geographical area you will be wasting a huge amount of time and not doing the important things. Too many players try to have perfect research.

Perfect research is not critical to this effort. We want enough information to give us a strong sense of what the needs of the Company might be and who the appropriate decision maker might be. Once this is accomplished, our efforts must primarily revolve around accessing the appropriate decision maker.

Complete Target Research. I cannot overemphasize the importance of targets. Targets are absolutely essential in this process. Targets make everything else we do more effective. It gives us a focus and a direction. Targets help us help others help us. It's worth repeating– Targets help us help others help us. Notice that this is directed by you.

The first level of research is to gain a general overview of what is happening in a particular region. The economic conditions in the Northeast are quite different from Southern California and areas in between. It's a good thing to know, as part of your decision-making process, which areas are really doing well. This is key to all decision making in *WIN THE CAREER GAME NOW!!* It is quite simple to do a Google search on growth areas and industries.

For example, some time ago a keyword search on Google for "growth industries Colorado" turned up a comprehensive 238-page study completed for the Colorado Office of Economic Development. It contains an incredible amount of detail on 15 growth industries in Colorado. The Internet has truly changed and improved research in the game an order of magnitude. It is simple, effective, and comprehensive.

After general research on geography and industry, the next step is to investigate companies in those industries in that geographic area. A search of Dun & Bradstreet (www.dnb.com/us/) or Hoover's (www.hoovers.com/free/) will give you an incredible amount of information quickly and easily. Yahoo finance (http://finance.yahoo.com/) is another great source, as are America's Career Info (www.americascareerinfo.net) and Thomas Regional (www.thomasregional.com).

One of the most current research tools for targeting is LinkedIn Industries. You'll find the industry directory at: https://www.linkedin.com/companyDir?industries=. After identifying your target industry, simply enter the industry in the search box at the top of the page and list of companies is identified. For example, there are 344,610 technology companies listed on LinkedIn globally, 94,288 in the United States, and 8242 in San Francisco. Incidentally in Cheyenne, WY there are 43!

There are many other resources and the research librarian at your local library will be a tremendous asset.

The research that we now have available allows us to learn more information about specific decision makers then at any time in the past. This is a huge improvement over what we were able to accomplish ten years ago. This allows us to find "positive hooks" that will allow us to differentiate ourselves as we contact the appropriate decision maker.

Once we have identified our target companies, we can then identify the appropriate decision makers. Our target must always be the appropriate decision maker. Many people assume that the appropriate decision maker is the CEO or President of the Company. As a CEO is at the very top of the career pyramid, he or she is virtually never the appropriate decision maker for 99 percent of those seeking employment.

For a recent college graduate, the appropriate decision maker is most likely a manager or director. For a manager it might well be a Director or Vice President. The good news is that mid-level managers are easier to access and speak with than a CEO.

Normally, they do not have screeners and don't have the travel or meeting schedules that a CEO has. LinkedIn is a great tool to identify decision makers at the Manager/Director level.

Effective target research will help you use your contacts more effectively when networking. Most people ask "Bobby, I'm looking for a job. Do you know anyone that needs me?" This should not be your first approach when asking for a lead. A much more powerful and direct question is, "Bobby, I'm very excited about telecommunications in this part of the world. I think there might be great opportunity at XYZ Company (or in XYZ industry). Do you know anyone who works in this industry or a company in this field?" This is a much more effective way to ask.

Unfortunately most players in the game ask the first question. It is a poor way to ask because virtually no one knows specifically of a job. The second question is much more effective in putting the odds of a helpful response on our side because everyone has information and contacts at some level.

Most people have trouble effectively asking for a lead or referral. Ask with a point in mind, goal, or target in mind. Your research will be incredibly valuable in helping others help you. Asking with intent will help you direct the thoughts in others' minds. Remember, it is critical that you not expect anyone to think outside the box. That is, don't expect them to think outside the box they have created for you—their preconceived notions about you. You must help them to create the picture of you that you desire.

Exercise 6: Target Practice

1. Where do you really want to live (geographic location)?

2. Think back to your exploration in Exercise 5. What industry are you most interested in?

3. Remember the Bright Outlook section on O*Net? (See Exercise 5). Remember that you might be more apt to

find problems for which YOU might be the solution in a growth industry. What other ways might you find growth industries in your preferred geographic location? What growth industry can you find that most closely aligns with your interests and skills?

4. **Find three companies** in the geographic location and industry you identified in #3.

5. **Find** at least **one appropriate level decision maker for each company** (see above). *Hint: LinkedIn has a very good search engine. You can often find an excellent person to target by entering the name of the company and location.* If you could not find the target person you had in mind on LinkedIn, start with what contacts you *could* find, pick up the phone (or attend a networking event for the industry or industry association), and find out whom you could talk to about what's happening and opportunities in the industry or company (see p. 39). **Record** whom you found, their positions, their companies, and their contact information. **Keep this information handy to use after further instruction.**

Reaching the Appropriate Decision Maker

The "Positive Hook." The "positive hook" is defined as anything that gets you in front of the appropriate decision maker. The "positive hook" ideally will separate you from your competition in accessing the decision maker. It is a key tool in moving through the career search game effectively and quickly.

Any time spent in finding "positive hooks" is time well spent. There are little hooks and big hooks. A "positive hook" can range from direct referrals to geographic areas that the player and the appropriate decision makers share in common.

In fact, Len Gilmore, a former client and phenomenal sales and business development executive, used his "change" resume/letter as a hook to get more than one decision maker's attention, and it worked. I have had clients use geographic locations as in, "I grew up in Illinois and noticed that you came from there as well."

The only way to test a "hook's" effectiveness is to try it. Our ultimate goal is to meet face to face with the appropriate decision maker. Whatever "hook" works is the only one that matters.

Remember David's story. There are two aspects to his success:

> *One final note: I did have something in common with the CEO - we both went to the University of Notre Dame. However, I don't believe that is the reason he called me back. Rather, I did some library work, and saw that he was mentioned in "People in the News" in the Colorado Springs Business Journal. I think by acknowledging that bit of research in my voice mail to him, I projected a sense of sincere interest in his company, and an effort to be more than just another guy after a job. It surely made the voice mail more interesting than, "Hi, I'd like to meet you."*

David did his research very effectively to discover several "positive hooks." He found an article in the business journal that he tailored as part of his phone call. Secondly, and equally important, was his discovery that the CEO of Telephone Express was also an alumnus of Notre Dame. We will discuss these "hooks" in more depth shortly.

Let's take a closer look at David's background in regard to this appointment.

David was an architect who graduated from Notre Dame. He worked for a branch of Peat Marwick (now known as KPMG) in San Francisco focused on airport design. He had a young family with two small children and they moved to Colorado Springs for a lifestyle change. He had no contacts and no telecommunications experience whatsoever.

He did his homework, and discovered a growth company that was of interest to him. The "hook" will not get you a job; it will help you get in front of the appropriate decision maker. ***WIN THE CAREER GAME NOW!!*** is dedicated to getting you in front of the appropriate decision maker. You must take it from there and close the "sale."

Types of "Hooks"

It's important to define contacts and connecting with them as we prepare for making the telephone call. My definition of contacts is quite different than others in the field. I base my definition of contacts on the level of success in completing the call.

"Cold" Contacts

A cold contact is one that we know virtually nothing about and have discovered no effective "hook" that ties us to them. In the past these contacts came essentially from database research alone. As a result, "cold calling" is absolutely the worst and least successful kind of contact. The majority of job seekers does little or no research and do not attempt to discover any "hook" that might tie them to the decision maker and help them be more successful.

There is nothing worse than making a cold call without a "hook." Your chances of successfully reaching the appropriate decision maker are less than 1 in 100. Think of it, this means you will receive 99 no's. I know of no one in the career search game, especially those experiencing the downward spiral, who can successfully continue the process with that much negative experience. The already "unfun" game becomes even less fun and indeed could be considered unbearable by some participants.

The reality is there are many things we can do to convert a "cold" call into a "warm" call. "Warm" contacts will be successful 50 plus percent of the time. That means for every two attempts to speak with the appropriate decision maker we will be able to reach him or her one time out of two. This is infinitely better than 1 or 0 out of 100 in a cold call. I consider that to be "relatively more enjoyable" that a cold call.

"Warm" Contacts

This book evolved from a three-hour workshop I conducted for over twelve years with thousands of job seekers. As part of the workshop I demonstrated "live" the techniques discussed later in this book. When I began the workshop I was not certain whom to call. I went into the local business journal and tried the "People on the Move" section. When you think about it, the people who are in this sort of article are experiencing positive change. They have been promoted into a higher position or appointed to a board of some type. The "hook" was acknowledging their success and promotion. They appreciated the complement. It was that simple and powerful as a connecting request.

My definition of a **warm call** is a result of this activity. In over 500 seminars, I always set one appointment in a 30-minute phone session when I spoke with two decision makers. In fact there were typically two basic responses. "Well, thank you." And secondly, "You are the first one to call me who has not tried to sell me something." Invariably these comments were followed by, "Come on over, let's talk." This definitely puts the candidate in a much more positive frame of mind when making phone calls.

You can find "People on the Move" or something very similar to it in virtually every newspaper and business journal or business magazine in the country. This represents a huge untapped resource of contacts especially at the mid-management level.

(LinkedIn has put this process on steroids as far as discovering "positive hooks.")

If one of them happens to be in your target industry or a target company even better. These people virtually never are contacted for informational interviews. In fact, as you begin your campaign, I recommend you go back at least six to eight months in newspapers or business journals and find as many contacts as possible. This is an exciting way to turn a cold contact into a warm contact.

Other sources of warm contacts are associations. There are industry associations and professional group associations. They are both wonderful sources of contacts. There are associations for purchasing executives, IT managers, financial executives, sales and marketing execs and many, many more. There are numerous industry associations as well.

How do you find associations and when they meet? Once again look to your local newspaper and business journal. Many meetings are listed on a weekly basis. Naturally, the listings in weekly journals are not comprehensive. Some associations meet weekly, others monthly or quarterly. The *Encyclopedia of Associations* provides a very comprehensive list of both professional and industry associations. It will give you a very good snapshot of the organization and contacts at their national headquarters. Call the national headquarters and they will give you contact information on a local chapter if it exists in your city. An association President or Executive Director is a very valuable center of influence. Many libraries will carry the *Encyclopedia of Associations*, a three-volume set, in their research section. Obviously, you can find an online version of this tool today as well.

There are many benefits to attending association meetings. In general, there is a speaker who provides very useful information about current aspects of the industry. This is good. It gives you information that you didn't have previously.

Most association meetings also have networking sessions built in and that allows you to circulate and meet many people in the area that you are targeting. Your goal at an association meeting is to collect as many business cards as possible without appearing to be a "mooch." You will have seen them face-to-face and they will have seen you.

Do not spend too much time with any one person. A dialogue might be something like, "John, if you have a card I would really appreciate it. I really enjoyed our conversation and would like to give you a call next week to have a little more in-depth conversation." Then move on to the next individual. You have been face-to-face with the kind of people you need to meet. This is "focused networking" at its best.

In my mind, this is a much more beneficial sort of meeting then going to a Chamber of Commerce "Business after Hours" networking session. That is not to say there is no value to the "Business after Hours" networking. Instead, going to a professional meeting will provide you a greater source of focused contacts in the industry or position that you seek while maximizing the use of your time.

If you like the association, join it. An additional benefit of joining is that you will receive a membership directory. What a wonderful resource! These directories normally give you contact names, company affiliation, phone numbers, e-mail addresses, and more. There is also an excellent chance that one of these contacts will work for one of your target companies. At the very least, someone in that organization will know a decision maker in one of your target companies. In my experience, the success rate of contacting and meeting with these people can reach 80 percent. Four out of five is relatively more successful and enjoyable than one out of two.

I had a client relocate from Switzerland to Denver who used associations very effectively. He had been a Director of Information Systems for a bank in Switzerland. This bank used Sun workstations. He discovered there was a Sun Users Group in Denver that met monthly. He attended a meeting and the contacts he made led directly to his finding a job.

"Hot" Contacts

The most effective "hot" contact is a direct referral. Nine times out of ten with a direct referral it is not a matter of **if** you get an appointment, it's **when** you can get together. Needless to say, we want direct referrals as often as possible.

College alumni are second only to direct referrals in effectiveness. The good news is that they are a totally underutilized resource.

I think when people first graduate they don't need it, and as time passes they forget about alumni contacts. You may discover that your college or university has an online alumni resource. If so, fantastic.

For example, I am an alumnus of Duke University. There are 121,800 Duke Alumni on LinkedIn. My Masters is from Central Michigan University and there are 116,000 Chippewa alumni. Alumni are a large and typically underutilized resource.

For example, during the course of my phone sessions, I set three meetings with the CFO of a major manufacturing company in Denver who was a University of Colorado Alumni. I did not reach him every time I called (he was in meetings or out-of-town). However, every time I spoke with him, he granted an hour appointment. He gave referrals appropriately.

Incredibly busy people will spend time helping us through the Career Game. And, if your "positive hook" is strong enough, busy people will spend time with you and help you through the process.

Thanks to the Internet and LinkedIn in particular, you can almost always find a decision maker or contact of some type in your target company. In fact, with LinkedIn you can almost always find an appropriate decision maker in a company by focusing on titles and key words.

I really dislike not having any contacts at all when calling. If you call a company and ask, "Who is the VP of Marketing?" You will receive the question, "Why do you want to know?" Asking that kind of question puts you on the defensive immediately.

Try this as a work-around: I have an imaginary friend by the name of Ed McDonald. He is a truly multifaceted, incredibly dynamic individual who has worked for thousands of companies. Therefore, when the corporate receptionist says, "Good morning this is XYZ Corp. How may I help you?" I say, "I would like to speak to Ed McDonald." She will respond, "I'm sorry we don't have an Ed McDonald here." You then say, "I must be the victim of misinformation again. I thought he was your Vice President of Marketing. If he is not the Vice President of Marketing could you tell me who is?" This approach will get you the contact information you seek a majority of the time!

Natural Law # 4: Understand the Tools

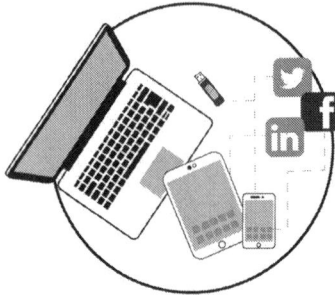

Focused Networking/Connecting

A few years ago Bill Morin, the then chairman of Drake Beam and Morin, said in an article in the *Wall Street Journal,* "I know I am saying something blasphemous, but there's a real backlash against networking because it has been so overworked." I really enjoy reading comments like this in various media sources because they are absolutely not correct.

The kind of networking that Bill Moran speaks of is not focused networking. The networkers don't understand how to correctly ask for help. As a result they hurt themselves and others in the process. Moran also states in the article that only 60 percent of jobs today are found through networking, down from 80 percent. In my mind, a 60 percent success rate is still pretty phenomenal.

The problem with networking today is that people don't understand the "realities" of networking. Networking is more effective when you work with "positive hooks" to begin your effort. Remember, your purpose is to win the career search game. Mastery of your reality and reason will help you focus your teammates.

The next two paragraphs are worth repeating:

Effective target research will help you use your contacts more effectively when networking. *Most people ask, "Bobby, I'm looking for a job. Do you know anyone that needs me?"* This should not be your first approach when asking for a lead. *A much more powerful and direct question is,*

"Bobby, I'm very excited about telecommunications in this part of the world. I think there might be great opportunity at XYZ Company (or in XYZ industry). Do you know anyone who works in this industry or a company in this field?" This is a much more effective way to ask.

Unfortunately most players in the game ask the first question. It is a poor way to ask because virtually no one knows specifically of a job. The second question is much more effective in putting the odds of a helpful response on our side because everyone has information and contacts at some level.

Most people have trouble effectively asking for a lead or referral. Ask with a point, goal, or target in mind. Your research will be incredibly valuable in helping others help you. Asking with intent will help you direct the thoughts in others' minds. Remember, it is critical that you not expect anyone to think outside the box. That is, don't expect them to think outside the box they have created for you.

King Solomon, reputed to be one of the wisest men of all times, gives us wonderful advice in Ecclesiastes 4:9-12 when he says:

Two can accomplish more than twice as much as one, for the results can be much better. If one falls, the other pulls him up; but if a man falls when he is alone, he's in trouble. And one standing alone can be attacked and defeated, but two can stand back-to-back and conquer; three is even better, for a braided cord is not easily broken.

This is true in so many ways. It certainly is the essence of what we strive to do with focused networking. Your goal is to recruit a team that will help you move through this process. The thoughts of Ecclesiastes give us guidance in this respect. The braided cord analogy is powerful and exactly the goal of focused networking, i.e. build a team that cannot be broken. Your teammates will be found in numerous places. They are waiting for you to ask them to help. You are the captain of the team and you must direct the effort.

In David's example after his hire, his immediate supervisor said, "You know David, you weren't my first choice. But John liked you." John was the CEO. David obviously had enrolled the CEO on his team. That is truly the object of focused networking. The CEO recognized that D.W. had functional and transferable skills and abilities that would be of great value to his company.

Mike Land is another good example of a really sharp operations manager with strong functional and transferable skills and abilities. With no college education, he worked his way up through operations at a local entertainment facility. He moved to California and ran a regional office for a national security company with a budget of $75M and 230 staff. The company went bankrupt and he came back to Colorado. He said, "I want to get into telecommunications!" No experience, no degree. He networked his way into the Antec Corporation. He found out what their needs were and began as a Marketing Manager and was quickly promoted to Vice President.

How did he do this? Because he was "wired" with functional, transferable skills and abilities and the ability to relate to and speak intelligently with key decision makers to demonstrate that he could solve their problems.

Try not to let anyone make connections for you. Why? They cannot tell your story as well as you can and they will invariably present you as someone looking for a job. Remember, in focused networking you are looking for information and contacts. Not a job.

When someone says, "Send me your resume and I'll circulate it for you," they are trying to be helpful. My recommendation is to respond," I really appreciate that but if you have three or four people you feel would be worthwhile contacts, I'll be happy call them and I'll let you know what I find out." Now what have we done? We've maintained control of the networking process.

If someone says they will help you, I believe they will. However, they cannot tell your story as well as you can, ever. I actually prefer to have the permission to use their name as a referral source (hot contact). It will save you huge amounts of time and frustration by being able to go directly to the contact. You are actually doing the referrer a favor, because they don't have to take the time to call and do any follow-up. As always, try and maintain as much control of the process as you can.

Using the Phone

The purpose of the phone call is to set an appointment, not to "visit" on the phone. Our goal is a short face-to-face interview with the appropriate decision maker, in their office, to learn about their industry and find out where you fit. Not **if** you fit, but **where** you fit.

You cannot build rapport on the telephone. It is not possible. You can get information on the telephone, you cannot build rapport. There is only one way to do it and that is face to face. Rapport building is what this process is all about.

The phone is the tool that will get you face-to-face with the appropriate decision maker more quickly than any other tool. Be aware that it is possible to "visit" on the phone with the decision maker. Don't fall for the temptation to "visit" with the decision maker on the telephone. Close for the appointment as quickly as possible and hang up the phone. They will never really know you on the telephone. You must get face to face. You will always get more information and referrals when you are face-to-face. You will also add a new member to your team.

The average informational interview will last anywhere from 45 to 60 minutes and has gone up to 2 1/2 hours. The length of the informational interview is the decision maker's choice.

In the midst of the interview, do not ever look at your watch and say, "I asked for 30 minutes and 30 minutes has passed." When they have finished what they wish to share, they will let you know. That is truly one of the magnificent things about informational interviewing in that people will share information and an incredible amount of their valuable time. Again, the time the decision makers are willing to spend with you is an affirmation that people are willing to help; you just have to ask.

The second goal in the phone call is to meet in their office. Gives you a chance to check out the working environment and gather more referrals. That said, obviously, we would be happy to meet with them for coffee, breakfast, lunch or any other time they wish. The smart phone era has made getting referrals a very simple and straightforward process. Remember, you are an "A" priority to that individual only when you are face-to-face.

I was working with a very well qualified CFO client a few years ago and he had an informational interview with a telecommunications CFO. At the conclusion of the interview the CFO told Bob, "I did what you are doing about a year ago. I like you and your qualifications. Here's my networking list, feel free to use my name." He gave Bob 50 referrals at the senior financial management level. Quite frankly, it doesn't get any better than that. Bob never had to make a cold call;

every call he made was a referral. That's the goal of *WIN THE CAREER GAME NOW!!*.

To repeat, at some point in time, a decision maker will ask you for a copy of your resume so that they can distribute it for you. Try not to ever let your resume out of your hands. Remember no one can tell your story better than you. In reality a resume means "needs a job" and if the individual has no job opening the resume will go into "File 13" without a cursory glance. The bottom line is you have lost a key potential member of your team as well as the referrals you might collect from that individual.

My recommendation is to say, "You know John, I really appreciate that, but if you have the names of three or four people you think I should talk to, I'll be happy to contact them and let you know what I find out." Always attempt to take charge of the contact process. Because as you are an "A" priority to yourself you'll make certain you contact them quickly and not lose momentum. Every contact is valuable; we want to make sure we maximize every one. The only way to do that is to "do it yourself."

Preparation for Making the Call

Work in batches, 15 calls per hour, two-hour blocks. If you are "playing the career search game" on a full-time basis, I recommend you block out two hours on a daily basis to call. In this way too, you can work in batches and build momentum in your calling. As David said:

> *"Win and I spent two hours on the phone, completing about thirty calls, all intended towards informational interviews. ...Let me make this point: of all the hours spent with Win, with the computer, with the library, and with my own thoughts, these two were the most difficult and the most successful. Talking to presidents, CEO's, screeners, and even receptionists is difficult when you know in your mind you are pursuing a job. The script is invaluable. I found myself far more comfortable after ten calls than after one."*

Scheduling a two-hour block of time allows you to overcome your initial call reluctance. As David said, "I found myself far more comfortable after ten calls than after one." It will allow you to demonstrate the power of the "positive hook" to yourself. Once you have the belief in the "hook" you will be virtually unstoppable. Appointments will flow quickly and continuously.

As a rule of thumb, plan on dialing 15 times an hour. Fifteen calls may not sound like much but as you will be on hold and leaving messages, you'll find that this is a good rule of thumb. It is important as you begin your calling that you call continuously. For every two-hour phone session you will need thirty targets completed and ready to call. Never waste time in a phone session looking up information.

Looking up information means you will lose your momentum in calling and you must avoid this at all costs. No one likes to make this kind of phone call, but it is just too important not to accomplish. Remember "creative avoidance." It's amazing how much time you can spend looking up phone numbers if you want to. Look up phone numbers and complete all your research at night or on weekends. I repeat, in your phone session the goal is to call as many decision makers as possible.

I recommend planning your phone sessions two weeks in advance. Schedule them daily and alternate mornings or afternoons. These sessions can be changed, if required, but attempt to keep your phone time sacred. The rationale is that if you have an appointment with a decision maker either in the morning or in the afternoon you will find an excuse for not making the calls. Two-hour phone sessions on a consistent basis are an "A" priority at all times.

Keeping Score

||||| ||

Keeping score is a very simple and important process. Most clients are amazed at how few decision makers they actually contact in a phone session. It's very easy to confuse calls with contacts. I use columns headed with Calls, Contacts, Voicemail, Decision Makers, and Appointments.

Calls	Contact	Voicemail	Decision Maker	Appointment

A **call** occurs every time you dial the phone number including wrong numbers and missed dials.

Contact is when you speak with an administrative assistant or screener or some real person.

Voicemail is just that: leaving a message in the decision maker's voicemail box.

Speaking to the **Decision Maker** means you are really making progress.

Setting appointments is what it's all about.

A good rule of thumb, at least initially, is that for every 10 calls you will have eight contacts/voicemails and will speak with the target decision maker, at best, twice. Of these two decision maker contacts, your goal is to set one appointment. As you have more phone sessions, you'll find that your success percentage will improve because you will find out when the decision maker will be out of the meeting, back in the office, or whatever. In the second and following sessions, you will be able to contact the decision maker much more readily. There is no way to skip the first phone session!

When is the Best Time to Call?

The reality is, **NOW** is always the best time. On your first phone session you don't know if your target decision maker is in the office or not, so call right now. It could be Monday morning, Friday afternoon, whenever. As you complete your phone sessions consistently, you will discover the best times to speak with your decision maker. By the fourth phone session, you will know when they are in and your results consistently improve.

Leaving Messages

I *never* want to leave my message with a screener. I prefer voice mail. This is not because the screener is a bad person, but the reality is, that she will not tell my story as I want it to be told. Remember "Gossip," the party game, where you begin at one end of a line with a short phrase or story and then see what happens ten people later? With voicemail you leave your message exactly as you want it to be understood. With the script we will discuss, you will leave the same message on voicemail that you will use on the actual phone contact with the decision maker. I actually consider voicemail a form of advertising and it lets the decision maker know that a friend or business contact has referred me to them. This differentiates me from my competition.

Have Your Calendar Ready

Schedule appointments in morning or afternoon. You will learn quickly in this process that your target decision makers will say "yes" to your request for a face-to-face appointment. Therefore, have your calendar ready! Don't fumble around looking for your schedule. I recommend you try for two appointments either in the morning or two appointments in the afternoon. If you schedule one appointment in the morning and one appointment in the afternoon human nature and "creative avoidance" will win and the chances are excellent that you will not complete your daily phone session. This is a fact of life in the Career Game. There are times you will not be able to avoid appointments morning and afternoon, but try to schedule two appointments in the morning or two in the afternoon.

Number of Informational Interview Objectives

If you are playing the Career Search Game full-time, set an objective of two informational interviews per day, three days per week. This goal may be somewhat of a stretch, but it is still certainly achievable. If you reach it, you will have six informational interviews per week. Then, from each interview you can gather an average of three referrals to other decision makers. As a "hot" contact, it is not a matter of "if" you get together; it's a matter of "when" you get together. It doesn't get any better than this. Done properly, you will never have to make a "cold" call. This is why this process is so powerful. When you're getting 90% "yes's," your attitude in the Career Game will dramatically change to the positive.

If your situation is such that you can only complete two informational interviews a week, that's fine. But make the commitment to do at least that number. It will take you longer, but the process remains the same. Gather three referrals from every informational interview and you will move through the process more quickly than otherwise. Now you're looking at 6 "hot" contacts instead of 18, but it's still 6 contacts you didn't have before and at least 5 of them will be delighted to meet with you.

Mechanics of the Call

Prepare and rehearse the script, even though the script may seem obvious. Say it out loud several times. Actors and singers always rehearse, vocalize and warm up. It reminds me of going to the driving range before playing a round of golf. In my experience, a bucket of range balls removes many mistakes that might be made on the golf course. By rehearsing the script, this forces you to think about what might happen as you make phone calls. You don't want to waste any contacts. In fact, why not try making a few "warm up" calls to friends or non-threatening acquaintances to get the vocal cords moving?

When calling, speak slowly and smile. Believe it or not, a smile communicates itself over the phone as "upbeat and positive," and this "positive expectation" will show (for example, you expect a "yes" to your request for an informational interview).

Make a note of everyone you speak with, most importantly the administrative assistant, secretary, screener or whatever you want to call them. You will want this information for your second and any subsequent phone calls. Over time, your goal is to turn this person into your ally. **Never, never, never alienate a screener**! Never, never, never try and go around a screener. To do so is to virtually guarantee you will **never** speak with the appropriate decision maker you seek.

Never be afraid to ask a screener for help. If you do ask a screener for help, it doesn't hurt to go to the very top. I had an exceptionally qualified client in the food industry a few years ago who was looking to find a similar position in the Denver market. The only contact he had at a major food chain was the CEO who had just retired. We called, spoke with the administrative assistant of the former CEO and said, "Yvonne, I really don't need to talk to Don, and I'm hoping that you can help me. Here's my background and, here's what I'm looking to do. Now who would you recommend that I speak with to learn more about what's happening in Colorado in the food business?"

In this instance, my client's background became part of the "hook." It made sense to the administrative assistant and she said, "Based on what you told me, I think you ought to talk to the controller. His name is xxxx and his extension is xxxx." The result: that referral turned into an appointment because, in reality, the referral from the screener was just as effective as from the CEO.

In all phone calls, take notes, be direct, and gather all the information you possibly can. You will be making too many phone calls to remember with whom you have spoken and what they said. There are many contact management software applications on the market and investing in one of them is a very worthwhile use of dollars.

The Telephone Script

The script is built around three key words: **help, learn**, and **perspective**. Once again, remember that our mindset is that people are willing to **help** you, if you ask and ask well. The information that you gather as you **learn** about their industry, company, and themselves is extremely valuable and makes you a better player.

Finally, we value their **perspective** on what is happening. It's that simple and straightforward. There is never a need to lie about what you're trying to do. You want an informational interview with the appropriate decision maker to find out what "reality" is in that industry.

The "unintended consequences" of this activity is that the decision maker you are interviewing really gets to know you as well as you know him, and becomes part of your team. To repeat, the decision maker you are with probably does not have a job opening, but the chances are that he, or someone he refers you to, is aware of an opening. Notice in the script that the first sentence after the introduction is "I'm hoping you can **help** me." It is critical that you use that sentence at that point in time.

When I began this process I conducted a rough survey of books in the industry that dealt with using the telephone to speak with a decision maker. I have extensive telemarketing experience and I realized that there was no way I could, in good conscience, use any of the scripts that were portrayed. Most of scripts asked the caller to possess a mindset that just does not exist in Career Game players. Some aggressively tried to demean the administrative assistant and get by with bluster. Others actually made up reasons for speaking with the decision maker. I realized that if I would not use those scripts, no one else would either.

The telephone script you will see in the next few pages is very simple and straightforward. Do not change it. Do not change the sequence.

It is the result of years of experience of other players. There is no place in the script for a conversation or a dialogue until you have asked for the appointment. This is worth repeating, there is no place in the script for a conversation or a dialogue until you have asked for the appointment. In general, you should not be on the telephone more than 90 seconds. The purpose of the script is to generate a face-to-face appointment with the appropriate decision maker not "visit" on the telephone.

Several years ago, Steve Rogers, a client with a director-level expertise in finance and accounting, mailed 100-targeted letters to appropriate decision makers. He actually did an excellent job of follow-up and received zero positive responses, no interviews. He was not happy, needless to say. In the course of working with him, I discovered that he had placed his value building statement before the reason for the call. The decision maker heard someone looking for a job, not looking for information and he had no jobs available; therefore, he was not interested in talking with the client.

We corrected his script and the next week, calling the same list, he generated nine informational interviews, three of which, because he was face-to-face, had job potential. One of these opportunities actually turned into a job offer and he took it.

This is the script. I know. It's simple. Keep it that way.

INTRODUCTION

To Screener: Hello, my name is (first, last name). Is ...... in? (Use John Jones or Mary Smith).

May I ask why you're calling? What company are you with?

SOURCE OF CONTACT

(Hot) Referral: Tom Jones recommended I give him/her a call.

(Warm) Association:

We are 1st level connections on LinkedIn.

I received his/her name from the ____University or Business Alumni Association or Society of ___(Accountants, Trainers, etc.)

And I've been doing research into the ____ industry.

To Decision maker: John/Mary... My name is (first, last name). (Contact) Tom Jones recommended I give you a call. (Repeat above contact info.)

REASON FOR THE CALL

I'm hoping you can help me.

The reason I'm calling is to learn more about the ____(high tech, healthcare, manufacturing, etc.) industry.

VALUE BUILDING

3-5 sentences, key points in your background of possible interest to the DM.

*I have ___ years managing, motivating, building teams of up to ___, an MBA, etc. in the ___ business and I want to **learn** more about what's happening in the ___ industry.*

CLOSE

*I was hoping to get together for a few minutes on next Wednesday or Thursday to get your **perspective** on what's going on? Would that be OK?*

Now let's discuss the script.

INTRODUCTION

To Screener: Hello, my name is (first, last name). Is ...... in? (Use John Jones or Mary Smith).

When the screener answers the telephone you respond with, "Hello, this is (first name, last name) Mark Adams. Is (first name, last name) John Jones or Mary Smith (whoever the decision maker is) in? Never ask for Mr. Jones or Ms. Smith, it sounds as if you don't know them and are in a subordinate position. This may be true, but we don't want to sound like that.

The screener will respond with:

"May I ask why you're calling? What company are you with?"

This is never an antagonistic question, she is merely trying to find out the purpose of your call and whether she should let you speak with the decision maker. She is the doorkeeper and part of her job is to be certain only qualified people go through the door to speak with the decision maker.

Our next response depends on our source of contact.

SOURCE OF CONTACT

(Hot) Referral: If your contact is a direct referral, you would respond, "Tom Johnson recommended I give him/her a call."

You have now taken the decision from the screener as to whether or not to allow you to speak with the decision maker. The screener has to assume that Tom Johnson is a friend of the decision maker and now it is up to the decision maker to choose to speak with you or not. If the decision maker is available, the screener will ask him or her whether they wish to speak with you. It is assumed that your referrer would not waste the decision maker's time. You will either speak to the decision maker or go directly to voicemail.

Voicemail: I have absolutely no problem with voicemail. It allows you to give your complete story without any buffer from the screener. You will use the script exactly as we are developing it here for the voicemail. In fact, the script remains basically the same for use with a screener, the decision maker, or voicemail. Remember, on a hot contact we are using the relationship of the referrer and the decision maker as the "positive hook" to get the appointment. The rest of the call is merely to explain what it is you want and that is always information and time.

(Warm) Association: "I received his/her name from the ____Alumni Association or Society of ___(Accountants, Trainers, etc.)"

If the contact is a "warm" contact use the name of the association as the "hook." The only difference between an alumni association and a professional or industry association is the number of positive responses. An association directory will provide contacts that will be successful 50 to 80 percent of the time in generating appointments. A college alumni directory will usually be successful 90 percent of time.

(Cold) Personal Call: "It's a personal call. I've been doing research into the ____ industry."

As I mentioned earlier, cold calls are to be avoided at all costs and are actually not necessary in today's market thanks to LinkedIn. Given the research capabilities of the Internet today, usually, some kind of "hook" can be found. Worst-case scenario, use the "It's a personal call. I've been doing research into the XYZ industry." Your chances of successfully reaching the decision maker are very low, but if you truly want to speak to them it's worth trying.

After passing the administrative assistant test, your next contact is with the decision maker. You will repeat the initial dialogue that you had with the screener

To Decision maker: *"John/Mary, My name is (first, last name). (Contact) Tom Smith*

recommended I give you a call." (Repeat
above contact info.)

This reinforces the "positive hook" with the decision maker. The next segment is the reason for the call.

REASON FOR THE CALL

*"I'm hoping you can **help** me."*
This sentence is very powerful and **_must_** not be omitted. Remember, a basic tenant of **WIN THE CAREER GAME NOW!!** is that people are willing to help. Asking for help does not mean that you are on your knees or begging. It is simply one human being asking another for help. You will be amazed how many times people will say, "I will if I can." That's just the way it works. People like to help, so we are giving them the opportunity.

*The reason I'm calling is to **learn** more about the ____ (high tech, healthcare, manufacturing, etc.) industry.*
The reason for the call is quite simply to learn about decision maker's industry. As

© 2015, 2016 Catalyst Career Solutions, LLC

115

we have discussed this information is
incredibly valuable.

VALUE BUILDING

Compose three to five sentences: key points in
your background of possible interest to the
decision maker (tailor your Value Statement
from Exercise 3.

The value building statement is a concise,
three to five sentence, statement of key points
in your background that will be of possible
interest to your decision maker and
demonstrate that you are knowledgeable and a
professional. It is not meant to be a
comprehensive statement of your background.

You will note that we repeat, "**learn**" again.
You actually cannot use "**help, learn,** or
perspective" too often.

*I have ____ years managing, motivating, building
teams of up to ___, an MBA, etc. in the ____
business and I want to **learn** more about what's
happening in the ____ industry.*

**It is critical that you do not stop between
the value building statement and the close.**

**Don't take a breath, don't pause. If you
stop after the value building statement they
will start talking. We don't want that to
happen. Make a huge note to yourself on
your script, "do not pause."**

CLOSE

*I was hoping to get together for a few minutes
on next Wednesday or Thursday to get your
perspective on what's happening. Would that
be OK?*

**The entire script should not last more than
a minute and a half.** If you analyze the flow
of the script, (remember it is basically a
monologue, not a dialogue), you will see that
we have moved from an attention step in using
the "positive hook," used the word "help," told
them the reason for our call, given them a
short introduction to us, and finally, asked for
the close or the appointment. They are feeling
positively about us because we haven't given
them any negatives to think about. It's a
positive referral, the opportunity to help us, a
little relevant background, and asking for a
short bit of their time.

As with all human beings, we tend to remember what we heard last. What they heard last was, "I was hoping to get together next Wednesday or Thursday, would that be OK? I want them looking at their schedule to see which one of those days work. I do not want them to try and help me on the telephone. The goal is an appointment face-to-face. It is worth repeating, never stop between the value building statement and the close.

It is so comfortable to stop between the value building statement and the close. People will be delighted to help you on the phone right then if you allow them. The absolute truth is that you can't build rapport or build your team on the telephone. You can gather information, but we want rapport building.

Remember David's interview with the CEO:

> *The informational interview was supposed to be just that; I was an architect talking to a telecommunications company. I thought*

there would be no common ground. However, when talking to the CEO, not only do you find out about all opportunities within the company, you may even convince him or her to create new ones. The latter was my opportunity. My department staffing skills and significant computer experience became as attractive a contribution to telecommunications as they were to airport planning. After thirty minutes of sizing each other up, the CEO and I were walking down the hall to meet the director of corporate development. After 30 minutes with the director of corporate development, I was going to lunch with the director of customer service. After lunch, I was brought back to schedule interviews with the call center staffing supervisor and director of technical support. All of these interviews were my opportunity to sell these individuals on a position that the CEO and I had patched together just hours earlier.

David had functional, transferable, skills and abilities that were a value to that growing company. Because he was face-to-face and listened and learned, he was able to convince the decision maker that he would be a valuable addition to his team.

Overcoming Objections

If you have developed the appropriate "positive hook" there are few objections to worry about. Objections occur only on "cold" calls. They are:

"May I ask who you are with?"

If you have a "hot" contact, this question will normally not arise. The fact that the personal friend of the decision maker has referred you takes the decision from the screener. Except for contact at the highest corporate levels, you will normally get through immediately

"Are you looking for a job?"

"I am in the midst of a career search, but I was hoping to speak with _____ (decision maker) to **learn** more about the ___ industry." A "job" is flipping burgers at Wendy's; a job is something you do at night to pay bills while you find your career. You are in the midst of a career search not a job search. So what you are saying here is absolutely accurate and true. You want to learn about what's happening because there is great value in it. Again, with a "warm or hot" contact this objection will not normally occur. If it does, just use the above response and move on. It is true.

"You need to be talking to HR."

When a screener says, "you need to speak with human resources," you are in trouble. It means your "hook" is not good enough. You can only respond, "Well, I appreciate the thought, but I've found that HR doesn't have the kind of industry information that I'm looking for." It's true. They don't. The only time I really want to talk to a human resources professional is if the Human Resources Department is my goal. Therefore, if you find yourself shuffled to human resources you must begin again. Find another hook.

"I'm not sure how I can help you."

I'm looking for the kind of information that only someone in the _____ industry can provide.

Understand the **"How, Who, What, Where, Why and How."** Once you have found a job opportunity, you can't control their decision to hire you or someone else. My goal has been to give you techniques and tools to maximize your odds of winning but you can't control the hiring process.

The goal of ***WIN THE CAREEER GAME NOW!!*** is to give you access to the "appropriate decision maker." Maximizing the opportunity in being with the appropriate decision maker is your responsibility. Therefore, it's important that you understand the Informational Interview. Wonderful things can happen when you're speaking with the person who matters in hiring. This cannot be accomplished on paper. Focused networking and the phone will get you the meeting with the decision maker. The unintended consequence of being in the meeting is that you might strike a chord that says," I need this person." That is what it's all about. When that happens, you don't have to worry about Human Resources or detailed job descriptions. Remember David's story. If the decision maker feels you "heal his pain" you are in. That's what this is about.

Exercise 7: Target Practice II: Perfecting Your Aim

1. Pull out your list from Exercise 6. Do you still feel these are good contacts?
2. If so, proceed with The Script and make your calls to set up your informational interviews.
3. Or, using the techniques in this section, get the contact information for the people you really want to talk to.

4. Practice your script out loud a few times. Have the script where you can see it; practice making it sound conversational. Nuance your speech with a little speeding up and slowing down. Use inflections in your voice as you do when talking to friends. Record yourself and play it back. Often, we can do much more with our voices (almost to the point of feeling silly) before we get to the point where we sound interesting. This self-evaluation and practice will help you immensely when you reach your target.

5. Make three calls using The Script and the techniques in this section.

6. **Evaluate.** How did it go? How did you feel? Did the calls get progressively easier? Which parts of the technique do you feel you need to pay closer attention to?

7. Now that you're in at least knee-deep, use the techniques in this section to compose a call list and set your Informational Interviews (which we will cover in the next section). Stop only when you have scheduled your target number of interviews.

For valuable resource tools and tactics to help you move forward in all variations of the Career Game, visit:
www.winthecareergamenow.com/resources

Natural Law # 5: Understand the Informational Interview

There are five major benefits of informational interviewing.

The first benefit is personal face-to-face contact with the decision maker. You are a real person; you are no longer a face in the crowd or a piece of paper in a file. When you're face-to-face you have the opportunity to build rapport. You've done all the third party research you can do and have gathered as much third party information as you can. Now you seek "real world" information.

The informational interview helps you identify areas of interest quickly and allows you to build your value more quickly. The information you gather makes you better. Why? Because you know what's going on in the real world. Even more important are the referrals you receive from this person. These referrals are this decision maker's best "guesstimate" of someone who could help you, either with more information or a job.

Use of the informational interview reduces stress. You are not looking for a job, so you don't have to worry about it. **The purpose is to gather meaningful real world information and get referrals. Nothing more.** If a job lead develops, wonderful, but the focus is on information.

The results of the interview will help you identify where you fit in the industry and who can give you more information (referrals).

The informational interview is a huge time saver. It allows you to use focused numbers as you move toward your goal. The decision makers you speak with will direct you in the proper areas. The benefits accrued from their knowledge are huge.

The informational interview is a powerful tool for a playing the game. It must be used appropriately and correctly. **If you gain an interview with a decision maker for an informational interview, walk-in, sit down, and then hand the decision maker your resume, you have just destroyed whatever credibility you might have had with that decision maker.** You might as well say, "I'm looking for a job, know of any openings?" If you will focus on information and contacts, people will help you. They will guide you through the process. Never expect anyone you speak with to have a job for you.

It certainly seems counterintuitive to seek information when you know in your mind you are looking for a job. The reality is the information that you gather from this person who is on the firing line is infinitely more valuable than any research you can gather online. It is well and good to ask a third party like myself about an industry or to do research online.

While I believe my view and the information you gather online is worthwhile, it is infinitely more valuable to speak to someone who is actually there. As a result of their position, they know what reality is. They live it every day.

In fact, I recommend that you **do not take a resume with you for the informational interview.** It is not a relevant document at that point in time. If the decision maker asks for a resume it gives you an opportunity for further follow-up. I repeat, **do not ever offer your resume at the beginning of an informational interview.**

The purpose of the informational interview is to learn everything you possibly can about the reality of their world. "I want to know what their problems are!" "How can I help them?

Your interview will stay on the right track if you imagine a list of questions–some that probe for problems, some that evoke positive responses. These questions will fall into three categories: Industry, Company, and Personal.

These examples are generalized questions that will:

1. Give you some ideas about the scope of your questioning

2. Establish the proper tone and approach.

Your own questions will be more focused and refined and more appropriate for the individual situation.

Industry Questions

What excites you about the industry?

Who is making it happen?

How are profits maximized: cost cutting, marketing, strategy, superior product or service?

What is driving the positive trends in the industry? Political, social or individual trends?

What factors are responsible for the industry's growth?

What new strategies are being used to continue the growth?

What are the overall earning potentials of your industry?

Is government regulation a positive or a negative?

Are you affected by environmental restraints? Are you affected by any interest groups?

Is your growth fast or slow? Is it typical of the field?

How about supplies or suppliers and personnel? What material supply problems are there?

What specific trends affect you? (Markets drying up, hostility toward the industry, cost factors, etc.)

Do you have too much competition, too little? What makes the competition better or worse?

Company Questions

What is the management philosophy of management here? How did that get started? How do you feel about it?

What's the management style? Open, command and control, matrix?

What are the long-range goals? Short-range goals?

What has been the major achievement of the company in the marketplace?

What makes your company better than others in the same field?

How are you attracting people to keep up with your growth (if growth is unusually fast)? What markets will you lose if you cannot attract people? What particular skills and abilities do you look for to help you increase your share of profits and earnings?

What influence do inflationary trends have on your business?

What are you doing to capture and keep your share of the market?

Personal Questions

There are questions you can ask to build rapport and uncover additional information about the firm. (You will need to judge how open the interview is before asking questions that might be considered "too personal" by some. Food for thought.)

If you could do whatever you wish professionally, what would that be? What would it mean for your organization? What prevents you from doing it?

What feature of this position that you are presently holding would you change or eliminate?

What development has occurred in your field that you did not envision in your career plans? What did this development mean for your future and the future of others in the field?

What does increased government activity mean to your profession?

If you had to do it all over, would you join the same field and organization? Why or why not?

What's the opinion of a professional you respect about your field's growth potential in the next five years?

What are your short-term objectives? Long-range objectives?

What professional in the field do you admire most, and why?

What is the most significant contribution you've made to your firm in the last year? The last five years?

What person(s) have you recruited who has gone on to fulfill the potential you recognized in him or her?

What attributes are necessary for success for a person in your position?

How have you changed the nature of your job?

Remember to rely on your natural instincts. They will guide you when you are in doubt. Preparation is important. Read, practice, think, and inform yourself. Then, in the face-to-face meeting, be flexible and receptive. "Play the ball as it comes to you." Actively listen to their answers, and take your cue from what they say to continue your line of questioning. It is in your best interest, naturally, to do as much research and gather as much information on the industry and the company as you possibly can prior to the interview. It allows you to ask better questions.

The key question for any decision maker in an informational interview is not, "Is there a job for me?" But "**Where do you feel I fit in this industry?**" Not IF you fit, but WHERE you fit. That's not looking for a job.

Don't ever get trapped by the question, "What do you want to do when you grow up?" or "What kind of job are you looking for?" You are there to gather their thoughts about the industry and where you might fit in it. Therefore, a very appropriate response would be, "You know, Brett, that's an excellent question and that's why I am here. I was hoping you could help me. I'm trying to learn where my skills fit in this industry and I was hoping you could point me in the right direction." **When the interview is completed you must ask for referrals**. "Brett, I really enjoyed our conversation. The information you have given me is fantastic. Who should I speak with next, so I could learn more?"

The more informational interviews you conduct, the better you become. You are building up your own personal database of real world information about the industry and the people in it. It stands to reason that the more people you speak with, the greater your depth of knowledge. You get better and more knowledgeable continually. As you move through the process, you will ask better and more focused questions of each decision maker you speak with. On the other hand, they will be providing you with more valuable information and also be able to point you in a specific direction.

Follow-up is absolutely essential in informational interviewing (and focused networking for that matter). Ninety-five percent of your competition will not follow-up at all. This is a good thing for us. In our electronic age, I would absolutely recommend a handwritten follow-up letter or note. It can be as simple as, "Dear Brett, Thanks for your time, I appreciate the information and your referrals, and I'll give you a call back when I have talked to them." This simple message is powerful. When you have spoken with the referrals you received, call the referrer back and let them know how it went and what you found out. Focused networking is a win-win process. It's sharing of ideas and knowledge and contacts between two people. Teammates, if you will. You will share the knowledge you have gained with them and that will make them better as well.

For valuable resource tools and tactics to help you move forward in all variations of the Career Game, visit:
www.winthecareergamenow.com

Conclusion

Play Well and Play to Win

Meaningful reality based goals will give you the drive and belief in yourself to achieve phenomenal results in the Career Search Game.

Duane Smith, another client, a mechanical engineer and COO with a medical equipment manufacturing history, mentioned in passing to me as we were working on his campaign, "You know, what you're espousing here is totally counterintuitive." I'll have to admit that focusing on information and contacts does seem unorthodox when what you want is a job. The bottom line is that it works and works extremely well whether you're a Millennial, a recent college graduate, a middle manager, or a "C" level executive. Just as importantly, it makes the "unfun" Career Search Game relatively more enjoyable. You're getting "yes's" instead of "no's."

As Aristotle said, "Adjust all your means to that end." The end, of course, is to win the "unfun" Career Search Game and begin the "Career Game," which is fun. You cannot stop playing; you must persist until you win. How do you know if you've won the Career Search Game?

Ask yourself these two important questions when you receive an offer:

Is this the highest and best use of my skills and abilities?

Is this a growth company and a growth industry?

If your response is yes, have fun! And quite frankly, I hope it is on your first offer. It is important to evaluate your offer carefully and not jump too soon. There's nothing worse than being in a situation 90 days and saying to yourself, "What am I doing here?" Accepting the first offer just to get out of the game without careful evaluation is a mistake." Why? Accepting a bad offer is just as bad as losing in the first place because you must "crank up" the Career Search Game again.

I admire Harlan Sanders, the founder of Kentucky Fried Chicken. Talk about someone who faced reality, used it as a strong basis for his reason to succeed and absolutely generated the result he sought. He was a winner who played well. Staring at a $105 monthly social security check, "Colonel" Sanders said, "That won't work," and he decided to hit the road with his fried chicken recipe. Over the next 12 years he recruited 600 franchisees and won the "business building" game, big time. What is even more impressive is that, after selling the company to an investor group and putting several million dollars in his pocket, he traveled over 250,000 miles per year promoting KFC until he died at age 90. That's what I call playing to the end of the game!! "It ain't over 'til it's over."

A Few Final Thoughts

Add up the rewards of beginning and the cost of neglecting to begin. Mentally add up all of the values, benefits and rewards that will accrue to you and to others when you "WIN THE CAREER GAME NOW.' Then, add up all the losses you will suffer if you don't try these tools and techniques.

Generate a sense of urgency. You know your purpose: "WIN THE CAREER GAME NOW." Exceptional persons produce under urgent pressures they have deliberately generated themselves. You now have the tools to put the "odds on your side."

Put your Action Plan together--now.

Build your team. Don't be afraid to ask for help. People are waiting to help you. Use your mind. Be creative.

When you find and play the "Right Game," you'll win. It's a simple, but not easy process of understanding your reality and developing your reason for playing based on that reality. Once you lay the groundwork, the results you seek will be yours. And remember the words of that Pro Football Hall of Fame philosopher, Joe Namath, "When you win, nothing hurts!"

Remember, when you win, all the pain goes away and it was worth it. Play to win... and play well.

Thanks for your time. I trust you found the ideas of value. For valuable resource tools and tactics to help move forward in all variations of the Career Game, visit
www.winthecareergamenow.com/resources

Made in the USA
Charleston, SC
14 November 2016